ODIN, LOKI, THOR, AND MORE

CHILDREN'S NORSE FOLKTALES

BABY PROFESSOR

EDUCATION KIDS

Speedy Publishing LLC

40 E. Main St. #1156

Newark, DE 19711

www.speedypublishing.com

Copyright 2016

For centuries, stories of the adventures of gods, goddesses, monsters and heroes have captured people's attention.

Long before they were written down, these stories were passed from parent to child and traveling story-tellers.

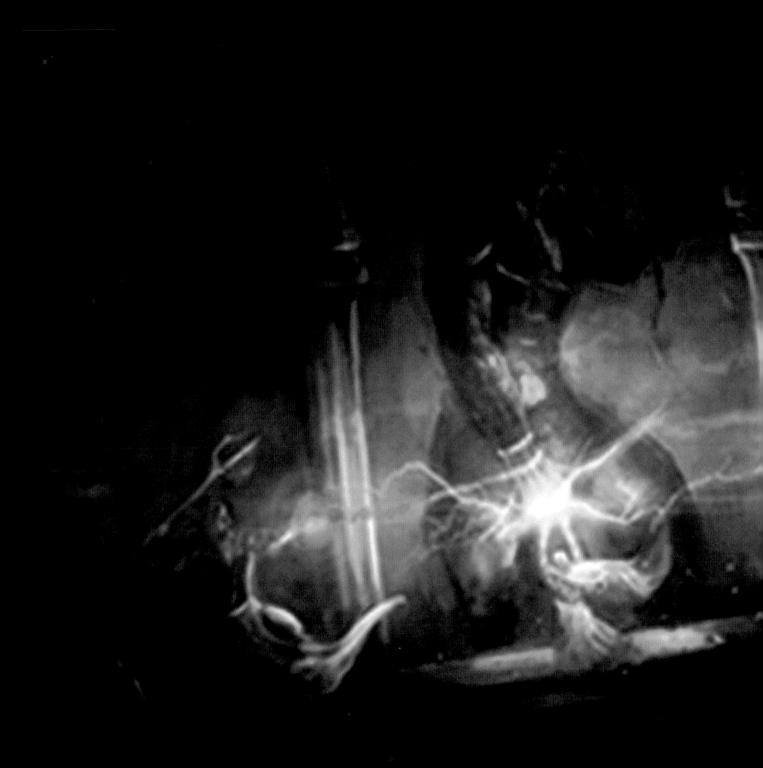

One of the most interesting and complex collections of the tales is Norse mythology.

It vividly details the rise and fall of gods and other creatures in a struggle for control of. the world.

With the rise of the Viking age, Norse people looked for stories of battle and victory. Vikings worshiped many gods and goddesses, especially those related to power and strength.

Three famous gods were Odin, Thor, and Loki. These gods were known for their adventures, which inspired generations of European folklore.

ODI

LOKI

THOR

Odin was the chief of the Norse gods, and had acquired True Wisdom.

Odin could see everything–the present and the future, all at the same time–with just one eye.

He sacrificed the other eye in exchange for wisdom. Odin was the most powerful god, considered the god of warfare and justice.

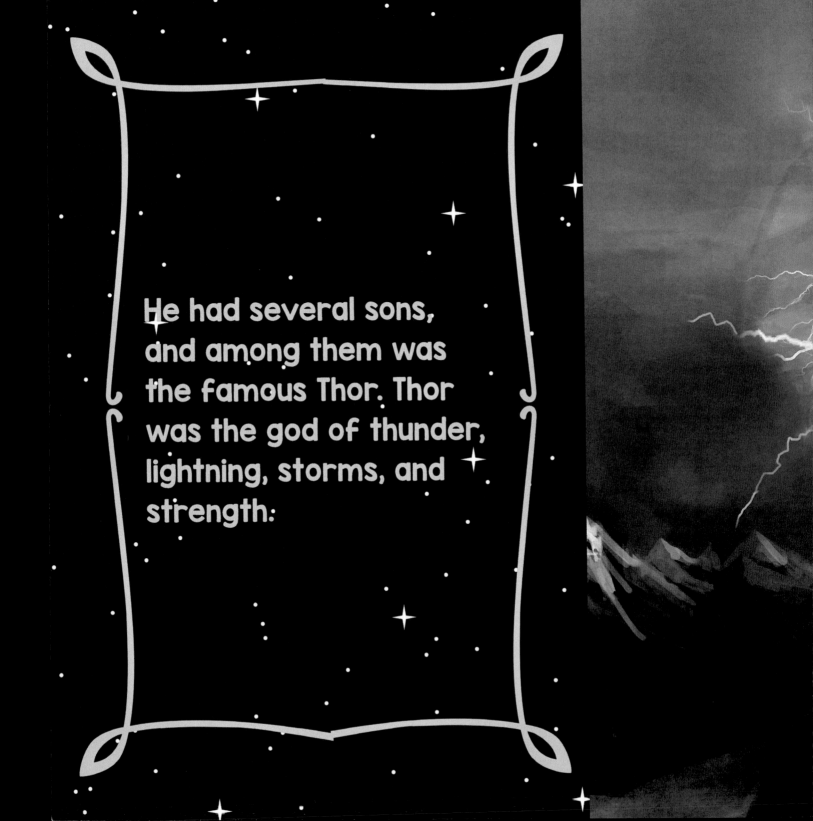

He had several sons, and among them was the famous Thor. Thor was the god of thunder, lightning, storms, and strength.

His signature and most prized possession was his hammer—the Mjolnir. The Mjolnir was the hugest and hardest hammer there ever was.

Thor used this weapon of destruction during battles, as he triumphantly defended the gods and fought with their greatest opponents, the giants.

Odin adopted a son named Loki. He is another known god of fire and is known as the trickster.

Though regarded as
one of the Aesir (the
principal race of Norse
gods), Loki was actually
the son of a giant and a
giantess.

Loki was the god of mischief and prince of lies. He was an archenemy of his brother Thor.

In strength and agility, Loki was no match for Thor. He was very cunning and mischievous, though, often causing more trouble than good.

There's a lot more to know about each of these three famous gods from Norse myths.

Each has been depicted and/or referenced in modern popular culture, in movies and comic books.

Go and read on to learn even more about the gods of the Norse folktales!